AF097837

my thinking
my lyrics
my songs
in the form
of poems

Copyright © 2022 LISA HILL

All rights reserved. No part of this publication may be reproduced, distributed, or transmitted in any form or by any means, including photocopying, recording, or other electronic or mechanical methods, without the prior written permission of the publisher, except in the case of brief quotations embodied in critical reviews and certain other noncommercial uses permitted by copyright law.

Hill, Lisa (author)
my thinking my lyrics my songs in the form of poems
ISBN 978-1-922890-04-7
Poetry
Typeset Addington Light 10/16

Photos by Lisa Hill and Josh Hill
Protest photos by Cafe Locked Out

Cover photo by Adobe Stock
Cover and book design by Green Hill Publishing

my thinking
my lyrics
my songs
in the form
of poems

Lisa Hill

For my sanity and the sanity of others...

Prologue

In this collection of poetry, you will find various topics ranging from one extreme to the other, with a lot in between - from minor, light and beautiful things, to dark, deep and heavy.

The writings have been inspired by short conversations or stories that were shared with me, throughout the years.

They have been inspired by the anguish felt by many, from various atrocities all around the world, as well as my personal life-and-death stories. You will find my perspective, feelings and opinion pieces on love, loss, injustice, inequality, human interaction, cruelty, depression, freedom, and hope for a better future. These are mostly topics that I was drawn to,

but I do also love our beautiful untouched wilderness,
and I wanted to include a few uplifting poems to
remind us to venture out and take in the sights, as
I do believe it helps us all to think more clearly.

Most of these poems are unambiguous, or should
I say (more to the point), they are not at all cryptic.

There are a few poems that were written
decades ago but are still relevant today.

And there are a few poems that may be seen
as controversial. I know that many will not
agree with the messages in these few poems,
but I think a little controversy shouldn't hurt;
and it should instead make this book a little
more interesting and thought-provoking.

My writing is my therapy. It is my way of
trying to understand the injustice in the
world, and to make sense of life itself.

We evolve and grow, and over the
years we think differently.

It is okay to change our minds.

Since there are separate poems written
over several years, you'll find a few here
that seem to contradict each other.

In a moment of sadness or anger, our thoughts are all-
consuming, and raw emotions are our absolute truth.

It is interesting, I think, to see the differences in our
thinking process at different stages of our life.

I turned my frustrations into writing songs and poems.

You will find that some of my poems are
short stories with messages within. I believe
we all have the capabilities to make up our
own minds about absolutely everything.

Critical thinking and the freedom to do just
that is important to me, as is free speech.

So, with an open mind, I hope you will find
something within these pages that will help you,
relate to you or inspire you, and maybe even
sway you; but that is indeed entirely up to you.

It is just. a book. of poetry.

With so much of myself in these pages, it is more than that to me. My thinking, my lyrics, my songs in the form of poems is something I'm ready to share. It is personal, but no longer private and confidential; I am wearing my heart on my sleeve and you will be reading my mind.

My new go to motto is: 'I need to be true to myself without the fear of judgement'. This line, which I read in a book, has given me much-needed encouragement; and so here we are.

Thank you so much for choosing this book of poetry.

A Little Bit About Me

Before you read
My thinking, my lyrics, my songs
In the form of poems,
Here's a little bit about me.
I missed out on a big break early on,
But that was before I wrote my first song,
So maybe
It was meant to be.
Maybe I needed to live my life,
To be inspired.
Aged seventeen,
I woke
In the middle of the night
With the need to write;
I had lyrics that rhymed a little,
And the very next day,
I had my first original.

I started to dream,
And that is all
It has ever been.
My focus,
My goals,
Haven't stayed strong,
But I managed
To write a few good songs.
I'm an unknown musician
With so many songs written.
It is time I did something with them,
So here you have...
My thinking, my lyrics, my songs
In the form of poems.

From Here

"Go back to where you're from!"
Some kid at sports day said.
At the time,
I didn't understand,
It didn't make sense.
It's strange
How I thought
That I was no different;
But the thing is,
Is that I was;
I was different.
It is strange
How it didn't faze me much;
But I guess it did
In a way,

As it's something
I'll never forget,
A distant memory now.
That boy didn't ask
Where I was from;
He just took one look,
And thought
I didn't belong.
I didn't understand,
It didn't make sense,
Because I was
From here.
I was home.
The only home
That I have known
Was here.

Perfect Patterns

Works of art,
Beautiful
And intricate.
Perfect patterns,
Made naturally.
Wind leaving ripples
In the water,
Leaving ripples
In the sand;
Colourful, shiny shells,
Pebbles and rocks
That sparkle in the light;
Leaves, and the petals of flowers,
The feathers of birds,
The skins of reptiles,
The insects, like ladybugs, and
The wings of butterflies;
All works of art,

Perfect patterns
To gaze upon in awe,
The natural beauty
Of our wonderful world.
Sunsets and sunrises too,
All gloriously different
Each and every time,
To remind us
That there is something
Fascinating to discover
In nature, and in each other.
Perfect patterns,
Even in our eyes,
Made to see
The natural beauty,
Nature in all
Its wonderful glory.

A Beautiful View

A short drive away,
To get away from it all.
It doesn't matter which way you go,
You'll end up in a slice of paradise;
Rugged country landscape,
Secluded sandy beaches,
A hike in the Adelaide Hills.
Wherever you go,
You'll be greeted with
A beautiful view.
The Riverland,
The wineries,
The quant little country towns -
Too many places to mention,

From KI to Yorks,
The Flinders Rangers,
The Eyre Peninsula,
Fleurieu and the
Coorong too.
What more
Could you ask for?
South Australia
Has got it all.
Wherever you go,
You'll be greeted with
A beautiful view.

The Shoes Grew

On a long stretch of highway,
On the side of the road
Is a tree growing a number
Of discarded shoes.
It started with one pair.
Someone thought they'd be clever,
I guess, thinking they started
Something new,
Hoping others would follow
In their footsteps and do the same.
I imagine that this someone
Would drive past once in a while
And see the pairs of shoes growing,
Not knowing who threw them
On the branches of the tree;
But knowing they were his kinda crew,
Strangers with the same sense of humour.
I imagine he'd smile, he'd be chuffed
That he started the shoe in the tree thing.
He planted the idea with the shoes he threw,
And that's how the shoes grew.

Your Favourite Things

The colours
Of the rainbow,
The butterflies
Fluttering their delicate wings,
The pretty pink flowers,
The super cute bunnies
Painted as a picture in a book,
Are just some of your favourite things.
A poem written
Especially for you -
Here you will read and discover
That what you see
Is the magic and beauty
In everything,
Even in the words
In the books that you love.
Dream and wonder,
Reach for the stars...
And live your
Happy ever after.

The Aussie Spirit

I see heroes,
And angels too.
I see them
Through the fire,
Through the smoke,
Through the devastation.
I see heroes
Risking their lives to save all they can.
I see angels
Giving to help those in need,
Who have lost everything.
Through it all,
Through the darkest days,
I see
The Aussie spirit
Shine through;
Through the grief and the sadness,
Through the heartache and pain,

I see the empathy and the sympathy.
I see the love for those who didn't make it through.
I see humanity at its finest,
I see the love from all over the world.
Through it all,
Through the darkest days,
I see
The Aussie spirit
Shine through.
Through the fire,
Through the smoke,
Through the devastation,
Through it all,
Through the darkest days,
I see
The Aussie spirit
Shine through.

Running Out of Time

So many ideas
Running through my head.
I'm not sure what idea to run with.
What is it that I want to do?
I feel as though I'm running,
Running out of time,
So busy working my life away.
Before I know it,
The years have gone by,
Not really doing what I want to do.
I feel as though I'm running,
Running out of time.
To break away,
Away from the norm,

To take a risk,
To risk it all,
To take a leap,
A leap of faith,
To believe,
To believe in me,
Is really hard to do.
So many ideas
Running through my head,
I'm not sure what idea to run with.
What is it that I want to do?
I feel as though I'm running,
Running out of time.

Never Give Up

There was no easy road.
There was no silver platter.
There was no ounce of gold.
He was going grey, growing old,
But he was still young at heart,
And he never gave up.
He never gave up on hope,
He never gave up on his dreams,
He never gave up, no matter what.
He kept on going and going,
And working hard,
Working hard up to the very end,
Up to his last breath.
Through the tears I smile,
Knowing he's watching...

Watching over me
And teaching a lesson
To never give up.
I know I'm going grey and growing old,
But I am still young at heart,
And I'll never give up.
I'll never give up on hope,
I'll never give up on my dreams,
I'll never give up, no matter what.
I'll keep on going and going
And working hard,
Working hard up to the very end,
And never give up.

I Told You So

I think and wonder:
What you think of me?
I don't believe that you
Believe in me.
I seriously
Don't think you take me
Seriously.
It's no joke
That all this is a
Joke to you.
I doubt myself
Because I see you
Doubt me.
Maybe you're right,
Maybe I've wasted too much time;

But imagine if you're wrong.
I will be strong,
I will carry on,
I will make you see,
Believe, and take me seriously.
Jokes put aside, on the day I say
"I told you so",
I will prove you wrong
For making me feel
Silly to dream away;
Dreaming of the day
When my dreams do come true,
Dreaming of the day when I say,
"I told you, see, I told you so."

A Novel Not Written

There once was a love
That grew apart.
Mistakes and heartbreak.
A love that ended
Was just the start
For other love stories
Within a story of one's
Entire life.
And so my life
Is just a few chapters
Within a novel not written,
A novel not read,
But a novel lived
And remembered,
A novel with sequels.
Mistakes
Had to be had,
And a love had to end,
For the story of other lives (like mine)
To begin.

The Goodbye "I love you"s

Dad grits his teeth and downplays his pain.
He turns white as a ghost; going quiet,
He closes his eyes.
I am suddenly overcome
With this feeling of dread.
Feeling helpless,
My emotions come to the surface,
Which I try my hardest to hide,
Especially from Dad.
Sadly, I can't contain my cries.
We've been waiting far too long,
We've been forgotten, while others
Who don't seem to be in any pain
Walk on by, into the emergency ward.
After hours of waiting, we get moved
From waiting in the waiting room, to
Waiting inside the emergency ward;
At least he's been seen by the doctor.
He's a little more comfortable, in less pain.
While waiting again, to be moved to ICU,
I sit by his side; we hold hands and he says,
Over and over, "I love you, I love you, I love you."

With only a matter of hours left to live,
He waited once again, he waited one last time,
The wait that was worth waiting for...
Until his whole family were there with him.
We were all able to say our
Goodbye "I love you"s some more
Before he peacefully passed away.
Dad was indeed loved, and he loved us back;
It went without saying...,
But I guess he wanted us to know for sure.
The only words that mattered the most
At that moment, were the goodbye "I love you"s;
And that for him, and in turn for us too,
Was worth waiting for.

Wish You Back

Tears fall down my face,
And it is all because of you;
And there is nothing anyone can do,
Nothing that anyone can do.
It's been years now,
But the pain of losing you
Never goes away.
I'm missing you.
Missing, every thing you do.
I miss you.
I wish I could wish you back.
There are times
When the thoughts of you
Make me laugh, and make me smile;
Then I realise
That these are just memories of you.
Will these memories ever be enough?

I wish I could wish you back.
If you were still here,
Life would be perfect;
But then again,
I wouldn't know it.
I wish I knew then
What I know now,
But there is no turning back.
There is no rewind.
There is no replay.
Lessons learnt the hard way.
There's no wishing you back.
Tears fall down my face,
And it is all because of you;
And there is nothing anyone can do,
Nothing that anyone can do.
I wish I could wish you back.

Mumma

It has been so sad
To watch you fade away.
These last few years
Have not been easy.
It broke our hearts
When we wiped away your tears,
Knowing then it was time
To let you go.
We want to remember
The days when you smiled
Your beautiful, beautiful smile;
When you and Pop danced hand-in-hand,
When Pop played the banjo, and you sang,
Always by one another's side;
That is how we learnt
What love should be like.
Mumma,

You are at peace now.
Not really gone, we know that now.
You will live on forever
In the songs that we sing
And the lives that we lead;
Because in our hearts
Forever you will stay.
We won't forget
You wearing the dresses
That you made,
And the comb
That you kept in your hair.
Being happy fishing
Or pottering around in the garden
Was your idea of the perfect day.
In our hearts forever
You will stay.

Breathe Easily

He reaches out to his wife,
And tenderly holds her hand.
"Are you okay, lovey,
Are you okay?" he says.
It's clear to see
she's not okay.
We keep our composure,
And fight back our tears
As we stand around in silence,
With nothing good to say;
Watching her fade away.
Suffering in pain, she says,
"I won't be going home, I'm sorry."
Which she need not need to say.

Our hope dies, knowing
She won't get any better,
She won't get well soon.
She's just going to get worse,
And we hate that there is
Little that we can do;
But being there lets her know
How much we care.
She tells us with each short breath
How lucky she is to have us,
While she struggles to breathe...
If only she could breathe...
Breathe easily.

Gloria

Being the good grandmother that she was,
She would always take care of her grandchildren,
As if that was all she had.
When they were younger, they would be over
Nearly every day after school;
And at times, she would sit for hours,
Watching them swim in her pool.
She has seen them grow
And have families of their own,
Inviting them all into her loving home.
Christmas lunch was always at Nanna's,
With all the trimmings, prepared with love.
Nearly every Sunday,
They would visit for morning tea;

She would make delicious scones
With jam and cream.
Her great sense of humour
Made them all laugh.
Forever
In their hearts
And in their thoughts,
They will remember
The one and only
Beautiful
And dear Nanna,
Gloria.

Baby Angel

Baby Angel,
Flutters
In your heart.
Baby Angel,
The light
In the dark.
When you see
Shooting stars,
Baby Angel is near.
When you see
Rainbows,
Baby Angel is here.
Flutters
In your heart.
The light
In the dark.
Baby Angel
Is near.
Baby Angel
Is here.

I Love You So Much

I can't think straight
When I'm thinking of you;
All that matters
Is being with you.
When we're together,
I go weak at my knees.
My heart skips a beat,
I love you so much.
Never thought I'd feel this way.
I want to be with you
With you all night and day.
You make me feel wanted;
That's the way I want to feel;
To know that you love me
Means a great deal.
I can't think straight
When I'm thinking of you;
Loving you always
And forever,
I
Love
You.

Husband and Wife

I believe in love at first sight.
When we're together, it feels so right.
There's no doubt in my mind,
No second guessing,
No asking questions.
We know we're meant to be.
You are my destiny, my soulmate, my everything.
You are my one and only true love,
Sharing so many special moments,
Moments that have brought us here today.
With our family and friends,
We'll come together like never before.,
And become husband and wife.
Here I am, living my dream
With you beside me.
Our love that's so strong
Has already lasted so long,
Because you and I belong.
Living our future,
Happily ever after,
As husband and wife.

The Best Days

To infinity and beyond,
A love I hold forever strong,
An instant bond with my baby boys,
Who have grown before my eyes
From cute and cheeky,
Keeping me on my toes,
To handsome, strong,
Good young men
Who make me feel
So proud.
The best job in the
Whole wide world
Is the job I have
In being mum to
My sons.
The best day,
Without a doubt, is
Every single day
Spent with them
Since the day

Each of them
Was born.
They are, and will
Forever be,
The best days
Of my life.
I am eternally grateful
For the joy they bring;
Grateful I'm the one
That they call
"Mum".

Twenty Years

Inspired by the book of poems read,
That was left next to the bed,
Here we were led...
Thank you for your thank you note.
"Snatching up this last-minute booking",
It was, among other words;
And so I responded with a poem...

Glamping in style,
One night is not enough;
Wish we could stay for a while.
Layers of rugs and pillows and sheets,
"Bayside Glamping" also brings
Rustic, aged, mismatched things.
Twenty years it's taken to bring us here,
Celebrating in a little style.
At least one night
Will be spent in comfort,
Hearing the waves in the distance crash,

Perfect weather,

Perfect setting,

Perfect simplicity,

A perfect way to spend our

Wedding anniversary.

A romantic excuse to get away,

To relax and enjoy.

Rustic, aged,

Mismatched things,

Layers of life.

Twenty years

Of wedded bliss.

Thank you

For a good night's rest.

Intimacy

Let go of your
Inhibitions.
Be in the mood.
Keep your mind
Focused
On feeling good.
Feel the kiss,
Feel the touch,
Feel the tenderness.
Togetherness,
Entwined
In motion.
In the moment,
Voice what feels nice.
Pleasurable feelings,
Coming together
As one
Intense peak.
Intimacy with your
One and only
True love

Makes
Making love
Beautiful & sexy.
Sharing your innermost
Intimate feelings is
A passion like no other;
Takes practice to
Please the other.
And pleasing
One another
Is the touch that
Lovers need;
Desire, affection and
Intimacy.

Picture Perfect Love

What you see may not be what it seems.
The picture perfect scene
Doesn't tell the whole story;
The fights in between,
The misunderstandings,
The hurtful words said in anger,
The tears and the ugliness,
The imperfections -
You don't see all of that
Because they kiss.
They kiss and make up.
The picture perfect scene
Makes everyone believe
That nothing ever goes wrong.
The fairy tale,
What dreams are made of,
Living happily ever after;
This picture perfect love
Is a love that has made it through

All the imperfections,
Because they kiss.
They kiss and make up.
They work
At making more
Picture perfect scenes,
And it's there love that stands out
And that is what we see.
A picture perfect love.

Split Seconds

Split Seconds
Is all it takes
For life to change;
Could be good,
Or it could be bad.
The problem is,
No-one knows
What the future holds.
Plan all you like,
But your plans
Could be put aside,
Taking you by surprise.
Surprise, surprise.
There is no choice,
You have to
Play along

In the dark;
Who's up next
Is anyone's guess.
Who knows,
What the future holds?
There's no warning.
There's no distress call.
There's no crystal ball.
There's no fortune teller.
There's nothing to brace you.
Split seconds
Is all it takes
For life to change.

Oh, Byron

We're sad, we're lost,
We're feeling numb;
Hurt beyond belief.
This dark place you were in
We now feel with losing you.
You know, we'd all be there for you
In a heartbeat, we'd drop everything
If we had only known
How close you were to the edge.
We'd pull you back and make you see
That life was worth living.
You would be okay,
You would love again, and be happy too.
The good times would come back
Around, and around again.
Oh, Byron, we wish you had reached out,
And cried out loud a cry for help.
Alone is no place to be when you're feeling hurt,
And thinking the worst of darkest thoughts.
There was, and always is, another way out
That we wish you had seen.

Your life will not have been in vain,
As we shed many heartfelt tears,
Knowing how much you will be missed.
Because of you,
We hug each other
Much more firmly,
Much longer,
Making us stronger,
Making us love each other even more
Then we did before,
Making us realise what matters most,
What we must do now
To help each other see;
That no matter how heartbreaking
And difficult life can be,
We have to believe
That there are always
Better times ahead.

R U OK?

You smile for a picture,
You laugh with the crowd,
You're included,
Yet you feel invisible.
Encouraging, kind words
Are drowned by your thoughts.
Your worst enemy is you alone.
It's you alone,
Minute by minute,
Hour by hour,
Thinking,
"When will it all end?"
You act,
Playing it cool;
No-one needs to know
How it is you really feel;
But there is an end
To your pretend.
You can't hide the hurt,
You can't hide the pain,
Not when someone asks,
"Are you okay?"

Let it
All out,
Cry those tears,
Have no fear.
There is no shame;
Our voices in our heads
Need to change.
Stop putting yourself down.
Stop beating yourself up.
Stop being so hard
On yourself.

The Game of Life

We need to learn the
Ground rules first,
Before taking turns in
The game of life.
Understand that
Empathy
Plays a part
In the game of life.
The attention seeker,
Who seeks all the attention,
Fails to see that they're not alone.
Everyone
Will have their turn
In needing help.
It may not be clear,
Quietly going about their day,
Hiding behind a smile,
Being strong for everyone.
Or it may be obvious;
Crying uncontrollably,
Crying out loud
For help.

No matter how we play
At being in the darkness,
One wrong turn,
Going in the wrong direction,
Walking towards the edge
Of loss,
Of no return,
Sadly, forever lost,
Is a crying shame.
There is hope in knowing
That there are winners;
Winners of
The game of life
Are those who make it through,
And those who do all they can
To help many others win too.

Heartfelt Vibes

Look at the impact that you have made
On everyone who knows you.
We all know how awesome
And amazing you are.
A cherished friend,
So kind and caring and funny too,
Which is why so many hearts break
Thinking of you, and what you're going through.
We can't stand to lose someone as good as you;
It hurts too much to think that way.
Stay strong, stay positive,
And fight to survive,
Fight for your life.
You can beat this, you can win,
We're on your side;

Sending you lots of love,
And big, big hugs,
And good heartfelt vibes.
Best wishes,
Fingers crossed,
We hope and pray,
That there is good news on the way
And that you're better soon.
Your loving angels are here for you.
We are here for you,
With good,
Heartfelt vibes.

It Kills

Think your bitchy words,
Your little push and shove
And dirty looks don't hurt,
You think they don't hurt that much?
Think again.
It's as if you've gone and hit her
Where it hurts,
Getting her while she's down;
Thrown sticks and stones,
Breaking her bones and
Stabbing her in the back.
It hurts so much, it kills.
How much can one take
Before you make them break?
How much should one take?
She tries to ignore what you say,
But your little whisper
Is like an ear-piercing scream to her;
It's on repeat, and plays over and over,
She can't get it out of her head.
It ain't cool, being a bully.

It ain't cool, playing along,
And liking what a bully will do
To make someone feel so sad
That they don't want to be around
Anymore.
Think your bitchy words,
Your little push and shove,
And dirty looks don't hurt,
You think they don't hurt that much?
Think again...
It's as if you've gone and hit her
Where it hurts,
Getting her while she's down,
Thrown sticks and stones,
Breaking her bones and
Stabbing her in the back.
It hurts so much, it kills.

The Aftermath of Torments

I wasn't about to allow someone to treat me horribly.
They cannot continue to be cruel and unkind.
They cannot think that their behaviour
Towards me was justified.
Criticism, free speech and opinions
Do not include being emotionally and
Verbally abusive or passive-aggressive.
You cannot expect anyone to sit there and take it;
To tell someone to "stop being a princess",
Or "harden the fuck up",
Or "grow a spine",
Or "who cares what they say?"
Only helps the abuser abuse some more;
It enables them to continue being
Demeaning and intimidating;
It enables them to bully and belittle.
How is it ok to let them get away
With not caring what they say,
Not caring how their words hurt?
To say "you're an emotional wreck" without
Acknowledging the reasons why
Is soul-destroying; it's as if your cries are silent,

No-one is listening, no-one understands,
No-one cares.
This way of thinking cannot continue.
It IS okay to stand up for yourself.
That is what we should do.
It is okay to stand up for others too,
To stand in the firing line
Of spiteful, cruel words, with the intent to hurt,
And say, "No, that's not ok. The personal attacks
Must stop! Stay on topic. Argue if you must,
Without being hurtful, without being cruel."
These toxic mind games are forever damaging,
Leaving us ruined, leaving emotional wreckage in
The aftermath of torments.
Understand that these torments must end.
It is not OK for them to carry on, not caring.

Ice Pick Horror

It's all fun and games, until someone gets hurt.
The devil within will do all it can to win;
The chip on your shoulder is wearing thin;
It's no excuse for all your sins.
Your short-lived high turns into a low;
Your fix only digs yourself deep
Into a dark, dark hole; digging deeper and deeper,
You lose sight of what's right;
Pushing away everyone who cares, who do all
They can to help you out; but to their
Horror you refuse you see them as the enemy.
In a frenzied state of mind, you take an ice pick
And stab and hack straight into their hearts,
Killing off every last bit of hope.
They back away, with tears in their eyes.
You ignore their hurt and fears for you.

The ugly truth is written all over your face;
This ice pick horror has no good place.
Only you can lessen the grip it has;
Only you can let it go, fight the devil within,
Fight the cruel, hateful thoughts you have of you.
Your thinking is all it takes to turn your life around.
There is a greater power within;
Your thoughts drive you.
You know what road to take,
You know which way to go, you know
This ice pick horror has got to go.
Bury it deep in the hole you've dug, and climb out,
Climb out and away from this living hell,
Climb out on top. This ice pick horror must stop.

Running Scared

They're wide awake and realise
It's a real shit frightening deal.
Battered and bruised,
He's suicidal and she's in tears.
Everyone they know
Has turned their backs, and refuse to help.
Frantic and desperate they knock on our door,
Because we're their last resort.
Running scared, running scared,
Running scared for their lives,
Nowhere to go, nowhere to hide.
An addiction has left him in debt,
And there is no way he can pay;
He's in deep and got his girlfriend along
For the horror ride.

It's like a scene from a gangster movie
Being played out in our living room.
They're anxious and paranoid,
Afraid they won't get to live another day.
Getting high ain't worth all the trouble and pain
Inflicted on themselves,
Inflicted on their family.
Running scared, running scared,
Running scared for their lives,
Nowhere to go, nowhere to hide.
This is not the way in which one
Should live their life.

Their Horror Story

He worked hard, away from home,
Having enough money to pay for things like rent,
But it was all spent on drugs and alcohol,
Instead of food and household bills.
The mother of his kids spent all their money;
With nothing left, she resorted to
Sleeping with dealers to get her next fix.
Getting wasted and high,
Neglecting their kids and living in squalor.
When he came home from work after weeks away,
This is what he found, emotions running wild.
Angry was an understatement; he was full of rage.
Using a rifle, he shot dead the mother of his kids,
And ended up in jail.
From neglect and living in squalor,
To witnessing horrific horror -
These poor kids were left worse off,
With their mother dead,
And having a father as a murderer.
A real-life horror story you wouldn't want to share,

To keep secret under lock and key,
Buried under tears of shame and loss
From an unforgiving crime.
Their only way through is knowing what not to do:
Not to drown your sorrows in drugs and alcohol,
Not to trade your body for evil addictions,
Not to neglect the ones you love,
Not to live in squalor conditions,
Not to lose your self-control with rage,
Not to murder or harm anyone,
Not to follow in these horrific footsteps.
Their horror story ends with them moving on,
Knowing they are innocent;
Knowing they can create a better future,
With hope for a life of love and happiness,
Leaving the horror behind for good.

Stepping on Eggshells

Quiet and reserved,
I'll keep my thoughts to myself,
I'll bite my tongue,
Careful not to offend anyone.
I won't reveal how I really feel,
Stepping on eggshells;
Uncomfortably sad
When I'm afraid
To speak my mind;
Knots in my tummy
Will one day come undone.
Stepping on eggshells,
No matter how careful,
A slip-up is inevitable.

Misunderstandings,
Misunderstood,
Toxic cracks
Will break
Under the
Intense pressure from
Stepping on eggshells;
Provoking
Explosive
Tempers,
Even when no words are said;
Makes me want to stay far,
Far away.

Not Anymore

You can take your cheap shots

And call me names,

Dislike me all you want,

It's all the same;

You don't hurt me,

You can't get to me

Like you did before;

Not anymore.

I don't care what you think of me,

I know you love to hate me.

You're wasting your time and energy,

Hating on me.

Read it here,

Let me make myself clear:

I've moved on,

I'm feeling strong,

Letting go of the wrong.

Believe me when I say

You don't hurt me,

You can't get to me

Like you did before,

Not anymore.

Wild Flowers

Where no care was given,
Where living wasn't easy,
Trampled on and all alone,
They survived the storms,
That pushed them
To their brink,
That pounded them
From above.
They survived the
Searing,
Heated
Moments
Day after day.
They survived

The harshest
Of conditions,
Flourishing
Through it all.
They stood tall
With their heads held high.
Being beautiful,
Like wild flowers
They grew
Where many others
Would have died.

A Loaded Gun

No matter what I say,
No matter what I do,
It's never going to be
Good enough for you.
I'm damned if I do,
I'm damned if I don't;
I'm not sure what it is that you want.
Going around in circles,
Around in circles;
I've heard it all before,
All before.
I repeat what I said,
Just to get it through your head;
Your sarcasm, your hatred, your negativity,
Your poison words are just as deadly
As a loaded gun.
You're a loaded gun

At war with everyone;
And we're dead to you,
As good as dead to you.
In your mind, everyone but you is wrong.
Can't you see that just can't be?
You make a big deal out of nothing,
Distorting the truth.
You must be confused.
If only you could wake up and see
How wrong you have been.
Why not try being nice and get along with everyone?
Because your sarcasm, your hatred, your negativity,
Your poison words are just as deadly
As a loaded gun. You're a loaded gun
At war with everyone, and we're dead to you;
As good as dead to you.

Beyond Repair

Cracks run too deep.
It's broken,
Shattered,
Destroyed
Beyond repair.
What was fragile
Needed to be handled with care.
The glimmer of hope unstuck,
Before we had a chance
To make it stronger.
It's strange
How we won't ever,
Never ever,
Try again

To fix what's lost,
What we can't replace;
It'll never be the same,
It's such a shame.
Cracks run too deep.
It's broken,
Shattered,
Destroyed
Beyond repair.

How We Used to Be

We did everything
Together.
Remember how we used to be,
With so many great memories,
Like singing side by side,
In harmony?
Now we're lost in the dark,
We're worlds apart,
Never going to find our way back
To how we used to be.
Blinded by the animosity,
We just can't get past.

It breaks my heart
How things have changed,
How we are not
How we used to be
Even after everything
That's been and said and done.
I wonder how you are,
And I hope you're doing okay;
Because nothing will ever
Take away
How we used to be.

Memory Lane

Sometimes memory lane
Brings us heartache and pain;
Best not to step back,
We need to stay on track,
And never look back.
Days wasted,
Too many tears shed;
Going back in time
Only plays on your mind.
Over-thinking what might have been
If things were done differently
Changes nothing.
The past is where it should be,
And that's a good thing.
Unpack the baggage and let it go,
Slam that door shut and never look back.
Live for today and tomorrow, and the day after that.
Sometimes memory lane
Brings us heartache and pain.
Best not to step back.
We need to stay on track,
And never look back.

Taken for a Ride

Careful who you trust,
Careful who you let in;
Don't be naive, or
You'll get hurt;
You'll be taken advantage of,
And taken for a ride.
Beware of the scammers,
Beware of the scum out there,
Preying on the kind and the lonely;
Who take the time to listen to their lies,
Fooling you in many different, deceiving ways.
Some will take the time to get to know you,

And pretend that they care;
Some will write a letter, and hope
You're one of the ones
Gullible enough to reply;
Others will dress in disguise,
Taking all you own,
Disappearing
Without a trace.
I don't want to see you get hurt.
I don't want to see you
Taken for a ride.

The Villain

Believing her lies, believing she's right.
Apologies, yeah right; that's not her style.
Smirks, rolling eyes, sly remarks,
Malicious intent,
Out to destroy her enemy,
Ammunition ready.
Manipulating others
To do her dirty work;
She was cunning.
No amount of words will make her realise,
The error of her ways;
Video footage, proof of who she really is,
Missed the part of her being the victim
That she says she is.
Her reasoning doesn't excuse
Her cruel, vengeful torments.
There is no excuse,
There is no condoning
Her spiteful behaviour,

Her lack of empathy,
Her misconstrued stories.
Declaring she just couldn't help herself,
Happy that she hurt someone else,
Has in the end hurt herself.
With eyes on her knowing, she didn't care;
She couldn't squirm her way out,
Trying, with crocodile tears;
There is no doubt that she
Was more annoyed at being caught out.
If it was all scripted, if it was all acting,
Then she played her part of the villain well.
The beautiful bride who looked so nice,
Married at first sight,
Didn't look nice in the end,
Her love story spoiled
For acting out and being the villain;
Sadly, that is the title, that she is given.

The Slaughter

I have opened my eyes,
And now I can't get the images
Out of my mind.
It is criminal, what goes on
Behind the scenes.
People know, but they don't want to see
The torture and screams,
The blood and the guts;
They don't want to see
The slaughter.
Brainwashed by clever marketing,
That makes us think that this is what we need
To be healthy and grow up big and strong,
But it is just so wrong.
Open your eyes and see
What goes on behind the scenes;
Tell me why
No-one wants to see
The slaughter.
Tell me why
It made me cry.

Worth More Dead

Tears stained her cheeks,
Her cries of sadness,
Her screams of terror,
Her feelings
Ignored.
She had a name,
She was
Supposedly
Loved;
But the love
Of money
Cost her
Her life;
She was
Worth more dead
Then she was alive.
In the eyes
Of her owners,
She was just a
Commodity,

And never free.
Led to the slaughter,
Her bloody end
Doesn't end there.
Taste the terror
And the fear
And the shock.
Her flesh rotting
In the pit of a stomach;
Each cut, each piece
Of her horrifying
Reasons for existing
Is sickening, and hard to
Swallow; it's hard to digest.
It's sad
That she was
Worth more dead
Then she was alive.

End the Pain and Suffering

We must learn
From the past mistakes,
Wake up and see it's time for change.
Time for evolution,
Time to do things the right way,
Time to end the pain and suffering.
Fed poisonous lies,
Grown up to believe
That that's the circle of life,
But it is not right.
Once we learn the truth,
There is no turning back;
It's not extreme,
It's not a fad or a phase.
End the spread of disease,
End the pollution,
End the cruelty
Which killing brings.
Seek the truth within the web of lies,
Wake up and see
It's time for change,
Time to end the pain and suffering.

Research the Research

It seems we all need to suffer at something,
We need to live through hell, grieve a loss,
Experience trauma of some sort,
Before one of us stands up and says, "No more."
There's a reason why someone so loved
Suffers and dies before our very eyes;
Testing times, life lessons,
A fucking cruel way to learn
That maybe we've been taught wrong,
Believed in something we shouldn't have.
We need to do our own research,
Sift through the conflicting information,
And know prevention is key.
We don't need to watch anyone else
We love suffer in pain and die,
Or believe that's our fate,
That's our genes,
It runs in the family.

Stop believing that that's life;
We just take it, whether we like it or not.
I say, "Nope, I'm not having it!"
Research the research,
And you'll find the answers are there.
Start with a book titled "How not to die".
Now I know what I know, it angers me
That the authorities that can make a difference
Don't tell the world about how we
Can save ourselves.
Life lessons shouldn't involve a cruel test.
Let's pay attention, take it seriously,
As we would if we were bitten
By a venomous snake;
What do you do? It's life and death.
Ask yourself why the one you loved died.
Could it have been prevented?

Playing on Their Minds

No child should suffer
From being abused,
From being used;
It's a disgrace they
Should never have to face.
It's been going on for way too long;
We all know it's so wrong, this can't go on.
Too many children going through
The same tortures, pain, all on their own,
Shocking memories haunting them
For the rest of their lives,
Playing on their minds;
Afraid and confused,
Suppressing the truth,
The mental scars cut so deep.

A childhood ruined, forever blurred
By memories that shouldn't even be there;
Memories no child should have to bear,
Playing on their minds.
A life-long sentence, the injustice carries on,
And they will never win,
Surrounded by a world of sin.
Haunted by disturbing memories,
Playing on their minds.

This ain't no child's play.

Sadistic Types

Sadistic, perverted and callous,
With no moral compass,
No empathy,
Forcing themselves
On someone,
And finding pleasure
In harming their prey,
Harming their victim.
Predators like these
Need harsher penalties
To discourage others,
To put them off the scent.
Lock them up and throw away the key.
Give them no rights and no freedoms;
Jail should not resemble a holiday,
It needs to be a hell hole
With no gyms and no TVs.

For serial offenders,
Bring back the death penalty.
If these sadistic types
Are free to roam the streets,
We are all in danger,
We are all in harm's way;
No-one is safe, unless the laws change.
Victims living with disturbing trauma,
And given a life sentence without a choice,
Need justice served once and for all.
Set a precedent, so these
Sadistic types
Know right from wrong;
And they do, because they hide what they do,
So they need to know that the consequences
Will be torture, that they brought upon themselves.

Peace in this World

No good can come from
Your hatred and anger
And heartless belief.
No good can come from
Your guns and your knives
And your bombs.
No good can come from
The horrid and savage beheadings.
No good can come from you
Using children as suicide bombers.
I cannot stand by in silence;
I will not be afraid, to say how I feel,
To speak up for freedom and equality
And peace in this world.
You can't scare me into
Believing what you believe;
It's made-up nonsense, can't you see?

There is no need to be so extreme,
There is no need to kill for your belief;
It's hypocritical, double standards,
And it makes no sense,
It's coward, savage, a barbaric act;
Your belief is hell, and that is a fact.
I hope you listen, and I hope you see
That there is more to life than creating
Unnecessary terror
And grief in our lives.
Be courageous and be brave;
Turn your back on this heartless belief,
And stand up for freedom and equality,
And for peace in this world.

Screams for Change

I just can't fathom how cruel people can be
Towards each other because of colour,
The colour of skin.
Time and time again, history repeats,
And here we have another anti-racist protest.
Screams for change, screams for change.
The crisis is a multitude of things,
Prejudice, discrimination, unjust assumptions.
Power in the wrong hands is dangerous;
It's dangerous when they can't see that everyone,
No matter your race, your sex, your class,
Your age, your colour,
No matter who you are, or where you're from,
No-one's life is worthless, no-one is superior.
Each and every individual life matters.

They matter, and must be treated
Fairly, respectfully, and equally.
We must unite for what is right,
Minds need to re-set, acknowledge,
Empathise and rise,
Put a stop to the unrest and do what is best.
Don't be racist.
Enough with the hatred.
Screams for change, screams for change.
No more segregation, no more them versus us;
We must take a stand, side by side,
Together as one, all humankind.
We can do better, we can. Reunite.

Smoke and Mirrors

Guilt trips, manipulation, blackmail,
Peer pressure and bribes,
Power and greed, control freaks;
The news is bleak, it's frightening.
And everyone is falling,
Falling for their bullshit lies.
And all I see is smoke and mirrors;
It's tyranny,
Smoke and mirrors,
Can't you see?
Smoke and mirrors is all I see.
Blatant lies and double standards,
One-sided, expert advice.
Who are we to question?
There's no compromise,
There's no compassion.
And you think that they care?

Mandate and enforce,
There's no right to choose.
Comply, or you will cop a fine.
We will be free if we do as they say;
Do as they say, and we will be free.
They take away everything
That is good for our wellbeing and mental health.
We're suffocating, finding it hard to breathe.
Scars, scars on hearts, blood clots, adverse reactions
That go unreported. The news is distorted.
This is not about health, and more about wealth.
Smoke and mirrors,
It's tyranny.
Smoke and mirrors,
Can't you see?
Smoke and mirrors is all I see.

Free to Question

Rejoice, for we are young and free…

Wrestled to the ground,
Silenced and gagged,
Cover-ups, censored and outcast,
Treated worse than criminals.
The pain and pleas and real stories
Are being ignored,
Making the days grow darker
With gloom and doom and fear.
They don't see clearly,
Throwing stones with condescending tones,
Sitting high and mighty,
Instigating segregation and hate,
Threatening our freedoms,
Freedom to think for ourselves and choose,
Freedom to argue and disagree,
Freedom to question.

No matter what, comply or not.
Either way, our freedoms are lost
Unless we rally together and make a stand
Against the tyranny,
Against the hypocrisy,
Against the insanity.
We will not give up until
We take our freedoms back,
Rejoice, for we are free,
Free to think for ourselves and choose,
Free to argue and disagree,
Free to question.

Fake News

The whole story
Not told in its entirety,
Just snippets
Downplaying the largest ever protest
In Australian history.
Exaggerating and focusing on things,
To make fighting for freedom look stupid.
Not interviewing the people,
To get their perspective;
Sonic weapons,
Rubber bullets,
Police brutality
Watered down,
And not spoken about.
Only two political parties on show,
As if the independents don't exist;
They're not seen,
They're not given the chance
To voice their opinions.

There is no open debate
Given to the experts
Who think the opposite.
Trillions of dollars are being made
With this scamdemic at play.
Fake news is manipulation.
It's a sales pitch,
Convincing at the beginning;
But the record is stuck,
A screeching noise
We all want to quickly turn off.
Pull the pin on the propaganda spin:
Fake news is now
on mute.

Murky Waters

Trapped inside the murky waters,
Going around and around,
There's no way out;
So you keep on going,
As if something different
Is going to come around.
But nothing changes.
Glimmers of sunshine
Brighten the mood,
The shadows above silence the room;
Darkness suddenly brings you back
To your overthinking, where self-doubt sets in,
Sinking feelings,
Crushing hearts,
Crushing dreams.

Grow up, just quit already,
Enough's enough;
Guilt trips working a treat,
Making me think I'm incapable,
Incapable to think.
I'm thinking now,
And I won't let you win,
So we'll see what the future brings;
Glimmers of sunshine
Brighten the mood,
Unmasking the truth.
Smiles will set us free,
Free from the murky waters
And the dark, depressing mood.

I Quit

Where do I begin to explain what brought it on?

Smothered, hidden smiles,
Breathing in my own poison –
I hate that this is our new normal.
It doesn't sit right with me,
Yet I'm the mask police.
I just can't breathe.
Headaches for days on end,
Feeling nauseous,
Feeling fatigued,
Pushing through the discomfort,
Crying on the way to work,
Crying on the way home.
I did okay, I kept professional,
Tried my hardest to fight back the tears,
Tried my hardest to fight back my anxiety.

For the first time in my life came
Panic attacks,
Hyperventilating.
This new normal didn't agree with me,
But I kept on pushing though,
Hoping the end was near.
The news reports unclear.
Panic attacks
Ending with tears,
Forced to take action,
To do what is best for me,
To take back my self-control.
There needs to be an end to hiding smiles,
And an end to shedding tears, so
I Quit.

Devastated and Distraught

Devastated and distraught,
I cried and I cried.
And then it rained and it poured,
And rained and poured some more.
Flash floods, rivers overflowed,
Entire towns under water;
All you can see are the rooftops of homes.
Currents so strong
Swept so much away;
Lives were lost,
Everything gone,
Giving me perspective.
What I was going through was nothing
Compared to the chaos unfolding on the news.
Devastated and distraught,
They cried and cried;
The force of mother nature
Unleashing its power

Gave no mercy,
No time, and no way out.
This natural disaster
Was a test perhaps?
To learn to cope,
To learn to be resilient and strong,
No matter how devastated and distraught
We are, we keep on going on?
Like the receding water,
Their tears dried and wiped away;
They survived to live another day.
What else is there to do,
But clean up the mess,
Rebuild and help each other through?
Like the clear blue skies,
We clear our minds and see
That we can make it through anything.

What's the Point?

Your story is so shocking,
It's hard to comprehend.
You've been dealt bad cards,
Lived through hell,
Then get given more upsetting news.
Hit hard, you take the fall;
You've got the weight of the world on you.
Feels like there is nothing you can do,
Nothing seems to go your way,
No matter how hard you pray.
You ask me, "What's the point?"
Well, hear me when I say...
You've survived this far,
You can't give up now.

Now I know how strong you are.
You have purpose,
To share your heartache and pain,
To shed a light on what needs to change.
Stay strong, face your fears head on,
Inspire others that they can make it through;
They can wake up from their living nightmare
Just like you have, and will do, again and again.
You've survived this far,
You can't give up now,
Now I know how strong you are.

Tyrant Psychopaths

A tyrant psychopath
With chemical weapons,
And nuclear bombs;
The threat of
Another world war,
Looks too real,
Too disturbing
To ignore,
As thousands
Of innocent civilians
Are killed, invaded, with missiles
Bombing hospitals and schools,
Killing women and children.
Russia's war in Ukraine
Will be a war against the world,
Crimes against humanity,
A frightening, living hell.
This tyrant is the devil on earth,

A psychopath out to destroy everything,
Power and greed turning
Coldhearted and bloody;
These atrocities must end.
No-one wants to see
Another world war.
Pray for a saving grace,
For a divine intervention,
A miracle, where the good
Outweigh the bad;
And the good-hearted people
Take over and take power
For a kinder future,
Putting a stop to anything
That is made to kill,
And putting a stop to
Tyrant psychopaths.

Cold Dark War

Newlyweds posing with guns,
Ready to fight for their country
And fight for their lives.
What chances do they have
Against the missiles and
Chemical weapons?
What chances do they have
To live in peace?
Against power and greed,
What chances do they have
To love, and grow a family of their own,
Against a cold, dark war
Out to destroy the very meaning of life?
Life is meant to be lived happily,
Not to fight in a war.
A romance amongst the destruction,
A love amongst the evil
Of those who just don't care,
Are newlyweds with hopes and dreams
For a future, to just love one another
And not fight in a cold dark war.

Laced with Greed

The brave stand up
For what they believe,
Not buckling under pressure,
Not afraid of being alone.
They won't cower,
They won't give in.
They push through the deluge
Of unjust and unfair judgement,
Up against the elite and powerful,
Up against the herd, who flock
To the feed laced with greed.
Money talks; it's a rort.
The lies will be exposed
For all to see,
And surely
Commonsense
Can't be ignored.

Truth, inclusion, choice,
Fairness and freedom
Are worth so much more
Than all the trillions of dollars
Made from corrupt handshake deals.
Mandate checks on the swindlers instead;
Kill the draconian laws
Ruling over people's lives,
And ruining our world.

Signs

Feeling anxious
Or uneasy,
Things that
Coincidentally appear,
That gut feeling
Might just be a sign
You shouldn't ignore.
Words you read,
You think,
Speak to you
Specifically,
Is a sign
You shouldn't ignore.

Keeping you safe,
Out of harm's way,
Are signs,
Literally and
Metaphorically
Speaking to you
Specifically;
Signs
You shouldn't
Ignore.

Made to Kill

Bloody massacres, murders, suicides & accidents too.
Over 45,000 dead in one year alone, in the one
Country, it doesn't take much to guess, where
firearms are their own worst enemy.
If any other product caused such
devastating fatalities, they would be recalled and
discontinued. Companies would be held accountable
and made to pay millions in compensation.

> The right to
> Bear arms,
> Weapons
> Made to kill,
> Failure to protect
> The innocent victims.
> Left behind are those
> Grieving a loss;
> They never had to lose.
> Preventable and unnecessary deaths -

Reasons are simply inconceivable.
Gun lobbies care more for money;
Their greed is the devil in disguise.
Pulling the trigger
To aim and shoot
Takes no skill;
Deadly and unforgiving,
A death trap
Made to kill.

History Lessons

Thinking history lessons were a waste of time,
Until you realise a familiar occurrence,
Where history repeats.
It is unbelievable that we haven't yet learnt
From the past inhumane mistakes.
How is it still possible that
Crimes against humanity
Continue today?
And I wonder how we can do better,
I wonder how we can change,
To make the world a better place.
Maybe history lessons are the answer.
We need to learn more,
Delve in deep and think.
Before politicians become politicians,
The subject of History should play a part;
Have them write essays

On what we can do to live in peace,
So history never repeats.
History lessons
On repeat, so we don't repeat
The inhumane mistakes;
So crimes against humanity isn't a thing.
History should be just that,
Ancient history;
Not happening again in the present day,
Not happening again in the future,
Not happening again, ever.
History belongs in the past,
Only to be re-hashed in
History lessons;
To read about in books,
To see at the movies,
To learn to live in harmony.

Family Ties

Falling down
The mine shaft,
Covered in dust,
And in darkness,
Losing sight,
With money signs
In your eyes.
Greed takes over,
No longer caring
About what matters most,
You dig and chip away,
Leaving love behind.
Wanting more
Than your fair share
Is not fair.
There is no price,

No expense spared,
On family ties.
Money wars,
A fight we should all avoid.
When greed takes over,
It ruins lives; it's not nice,
It's selfish and futile.
Cutting family ties
Is a cost that
No-one can afford,
A cost that in the end
Hurts too much,
It cuts so deep;
Family ties
Left to bleed,
All because of
Greed.

Not What Love Is

Love is not

Wondering eyes.

Love is not,

Uncertain.

It is not

About betrayal.

It is not

About submission.

It is not

Abusive

Or controlling,

Or manipulative.

It can't be bought,

It can't be forced;

That is not what love is.

You deserve better than this.

Better Days

I imagine
It must be hard for you;
What you're going through
Is far from easy.
We can see how hurt you are.
There's no quick fix,
No words can make it right,
Or take away your pain.
You have to stay strong;
The way you're feeling now
Won't last long.
There will be a day
When you will smile again.
There will be better days.
Step back from the edge,
Know in your heart
This doesn't spell
The end for you.

There are many
Who care about how you feel,
We want to help you through;
We see tears in your eyes,
Please don't make us cry.
There is no good reason
To end it all here.
Your story needs to be continued.
Have no fear,
Believe that there will be
Better days.

Remember the Good Times

I wanna reach out to you,
I want you to be ok,
I want things to be how they used to be,
I want you to see
How we can learn from the past;
Put the sadness and anger behind us,
Delete the text message wars,
Delete the unhappy thoughts.
Stop holding grudges;
What's done is done,
There is no changing that.
What we want is nothing stopping us
From moving on.
I know you think
That there is
No moving forward,

But we can,
If we focus
On the good times.
We did have some
Good times.
Remember the good times.
Delete the text message wars,
Delete the unhappy thoughts,
And focus on the good times.
Remember the good times.

Cutting Room Floor

Captured in our thoughts
And in our hearts
Are the highest of highs
And the lowest of lows.
Our minds edit out
The boring and mundane,
Magnifying
The turning points,
The heated moments,
The struggles,
The grief,
The significant parts,
Like falling in love.
The major snippets of our reality
Entertain our thoughts;
They entertain our family and friends,
They entertain our enemies,
And even entertain strangers we've never met,
Similar to reality TV, where they only show
What is most entertaining.

Some scenes ring true,
Relating to something we've been through;
Interesting to shine a light,
To watch from another side.
But the fact of the matter is that
Reality TV is manufactured;
Edited, with bits and pieces
On the cutting room floor.
A little like how our minds work,
The difference being that
The boring and mundane
Should play a part.
Giving us time to process,
And not dwell on our misfortunes.
Edit those bits and pieces out,
Leave them on the cutting room floor.
Think about what it is that you want,
And how you want to entertain your world.

Always Shining

Like a tsunami wave,
Our emotions play havoc.
Our minds are powerful,
Controlling our every move.
Our thoughts rule our world.
Swept up in a thunderous storm,
All dark and gloomy.
Lightning strikes
When we're not thinking clearly.
The warmth of the sun is always there,
A star that shines through all the darkness,
Dims now and then,
But it is always there,
Shining bright.
No matter how dark our thoughts are,
Our thinking can change
Dramatically.

When the dark clouds
Move away,
It brightens our day.
Even in the darkness of night,
We can still shine bright.
Our emotional state of mind
Needs to take a moment or two
To think things through.
No matter how destructive
A tsunami wave or a thunderous storm,
Or scary lightning strikes may be,
We all know they don't last long.
What is always shining,
What is always there,
Is gentle, warm and caring
Beautiful you.

Life-Long Friends

Never a bad word said
Between good friends,
Unless of course,
We joke and mess around,
Paying each other out.
Laughing out loud,
Fun times are always had.
With good company,
With life-long friends,
We reminisce,
So glad we met.
We know
Who we can count on,
Who will always be there
Through thick and thin,
To lend a helping hand,
Who gives a damn.
Smiles for days
Is what our friends give,
Along with hugs and love.
And that, my friends,
Is what life-long friends are for.

Selfless

There is absolutely nothing
She wouldn't do
For those she loved;
And she loved deeply,
With all her heart.
She went above and beyond,
To the ends of the earth,
While the load on her
Shoulders grew heavy
With every step.
While her world around her
Started to crumble and fall,
She didn't give up,
She didn't give in.
She would give all she could give,
And then give some more.
While walking endlessly
Into the dark abyss of
Relentless sorrow and misery,
She found strength.

Even while her heart was
Pounding out of her chest
In excruciating pain,
She kept on pushing through.
Through the tears,
Through the grief,
She made it through;
Her heart still had
So much more to give.
She was strong,
She was beautiful,
Admirably awe-inspiring,
To say the least.
A blessing for so many
She was, incredibly
Selfless.
And
She still is.

Sweet Old Ladies

"I'm coming, dear," says the sweet old lady.
I hear her shuffled little steps approaching,
To open the door, smiling. We have our usual
Chit-chat, before I start cleaning her home.
She sits in the dark dining room,
Silently staring out the window,
And I wonder how lonely she must get.
Maybe she likes the quiet solitude.
Once, I thought a retirement village
Or a nursing home, would be more fitting,
Where she can be a social butterfly,
Being a part of a community,
Knowing she's safe, where there is someone close
Who will check in on her often.
And then there I was, at a retirement village,
Cleaning for another sweet old lady;
And on this day, there was a wake
Being held at the hall down the road.
A procession of cars drove past.
"There's one nearly every week," she says.

Sadly, I thought, maybe this wasn't more fitting;
To live in a home, comfortable and familiar,
Surrounded by memories in every room,
Or to live in a community, with
Friends close by, and new neighbours too,
Who might not be there tomorrow.
Living a long life comes with an
Unimaginable, inevitable grief.
The elderly impress me with their resilience.
The fact that they keep on smiling
Is really something.
Having family and friends visiting often
Would make all the difference,
Giving good reason to smile.
Where it is that one lives in their retirement years
Matters the least; what matters most is living on
With a smile to give to everyone.
If I do grow old, I'll be smiling. I'll be wiser too,
More equipped to give sound advice,
Just like sweet old ladies do.

A Kinder World

She ventures out of the dark
And sits in the warmth of the sun,
Listening to the birds sing,
Watching the ants work together.
She looks at a web, and wonders
How long it took the spider to make it.
Like these everyday things,
Everyone is thinking the same
At some stage of their lives.
Alone in her thoughts,
She knows she is not alone.
These everyday things
Are there for all to see.
She sees that there are many
Who feel the same,
And they too
Want to see change.

The bigger picture
Of a kinder world
Is spoken, it's thought, and it's written,
And it is everywhere to be seen.
Knowing that there are many
On the same wavelength,
Who are on the same page,
Who think alike,
Brings us hope that
A kinder world is possible.
If that is what so many want,
Then that is what we
Will all see;
And that is what
She believes.

My Epiphany

When the whip cracks,
It wakes me up to
My epiphany,
Disheartened
That my all
Isn't enough.
"Maybe this job isn't for you,"
She says.
And she's right.
Being a slave
Isn't for me.
I'll escape
And do something
More rewarding,
More fitting,

Where my all
Is more than enough;
Where I feel appreciated,
Worthy, and valued.
I'll do something
More for me.
Thanks for
Waking me up to
My epiphany.

Who Wins?

What are we doing,
Wasting so much
Precious time,
Running in the rat race,
Working our lives away,
Tell me, who wins?
Getting things
That in the end
Mean nothing.
Might look rich,
But it's a poor way,
A poor way to live.
Why do we find it so hard
To get the balance right?
Doing what we hate,
Most of the time,
Running in the rat race,
Working our lives away -
Tell me, who wins?

A Promise

What I need

Is to be motivated

Longer than a week;

Take the steps

To get me there,

Resist my weaknesses.

This new year's resolution, made

On every New Year's Eve,

Is now a promise

I make

For myself,

A promise

I must not break,

A commitment to a

Healthier lifestyle choice

For the rest of my life.

From this day forward,

My cravings

Will be for something
Healthy and nourishing.
I will not deprive myself of
Something that I have
Wanted for so long...
To look and feel
Fit and healthy.
I will be strong,
I will not be weak.
Actions speak louder
Than words;
So I will do as I say,
Act upon it and make a move,
Sweat every day, to
Improve and transform.
My mind, body and soul
Depend on me, and what it is
I do.

Strong-Minded and Fearless

What are we so afraid of,
When the risk of regret
Far outweighs
The risk of failure?
We need to think more like an
Extreme sporting athlete.
They love the rush.
The danger
Makes it thrilling,
Makes it fun!
They push themselves
To do their best,
No matter the outcome.
No matter how many times they crash,
They get back up, and go harder;

They don't let the mishaps
Mess with their heads.
They're not just physically fit,
They are headstrong too.
Strong-minded and fearless,
They don't think about
Worst case scenarios;
The more challenging,
The more rewarding it is.
Racing against the very best,
Their competition,
Doesn't scare them away -
It inspires them instead.

Beyond My Wildest Expectations

I have a lot to say.
I have this need
To write down my thoughts,
This need to share my feelings,
To share my words, out to the world.
I will manifest my dream,
And make this a reality.
These words, written over the years,
Will be published poetry, in books
Sitting on shelves, in book stores,
And libraries, and in high schools,
All around the world.
It will draw people in,
Opening to a poem that resonates,
Leaving them wanting to turn the page.
This poetry book is a keepsake.

It will be something
Magical and beautiful,
Like a warm hug,
A message of hope
That no-one is ever alone.
Manifest, and my dreams will come true
Beyond my wildest expectations.
I will remain certain and brave
That my words will relate,
Inspire, and help.
If you're reading this,
It is a testament
That dreams do come true.
And your dreams
Can come true
For you too.

The Beginning

It is time to believe,
Time to do whatever it takes;
You can't leave it too late.
There is no room for self-doubt,
Follow your heart, and
Do what feels right.
Push yourself,
Rely on no-one else.
Only you can make
Your dreams come true.
Make no excuses.
Jump in
The deep end
To make a start.

The beginning
Begins with you.
Your courage and
Determination
Can make your dreams
A reality.
All you need to do is work.
Work at doing what you love,
Doing what you dream.
Make this
The beginning.

Acknowledgements

To my beautiful family and friends who love me for who I am, who have encouraged me to follow my dreams; and who have been my inspiration behind a few of my poems. Thank you.

I feel incredibly fortunate, having had hard-working parents who were loving, supportive and encouraging. Without them, I would not have found a passion for music, which led to writing lyrics, songs and poems.

My Dad bought me a bass guitar when I was nine years old and had taken my sisters and I to music lessons and was the 'roadie' for our cover bands. He was our number one fan; watching us sing in harmony brought tears to his eyes. My Dad is the reason why I want to

get my songs out there, in the form of poetry; I can
not have his aspirations for me, be all for nothing.

The poems - 'Never give up', 'A novel not
written', 'The goodbye "I love you"s', and
'Wish you back' are all about my Dad.

To my dear Mum, who has a beautiful singing
voice and taught my sisters and I how to sing in
harmony; I love you and thank you for all that
you have done for me though-out the years.

I have seen every thing that you have been
through in the past and it truly is awe-inspiring.

You inspired me to write the poem 'Selfless',
because that is what you are.

To my husband Brad, I saw you when
I was on stage singing, we locked eyes
and it was, pretty much, love at first sight.

Brad was the inspiration behind me writing my
very first song, at the time I was aged seventeen.

Thank you for all that you do for me,
'I love you so much'. xoxo

Thank you to my boys Josh and Blake for
giving me 'The best days'. I love you with
all my heart. I am so proud of you both for
being 'strong minded and fearless' xoxo

Thank you to my talented sister Anne, who
has collaborated on a few songs -

The poem 'Mumma', originally written as
lyrics by Anne and myself; was composed
into a song by Anne, which we performed
together, at our grandmothers funeral.

The Poem 'Husband and Wife' was lyrics I
wrote for my friends, Fiona and Scott; the music
was composed by Anne and she performed
the song solo; on their wedding day.

And the poem 'Oh, Byron' I wrote within an hour.
The words and the tears flowed. I asked Anne
to compose into a song, which she recorded
just in time for our nephew Byron's funeral
and for our sister Debbie and her family.

Cafe Locked Out - The work you do is simply amazing.
Honest, heartfelt and fighting for freedom. Telling
the other side of the story, of many lives impacted
by tyranny. Thank you. It has given me hope and
inspired the poems: 'Free to question' and 'Laced
with greed' (the brave - being the freedom fighters
and those who stand up for what they believe). Thank
you for the pictures of the protests and for allowing
me to select and use any photo that I wanted.

Thank you so much to the team at Green Hill
Publishing and Bookmark edits for the professional
and expert advise and work you have provided,
in helping me publish my book. You have made
me feel at ease. I am so happy and excited
to finally see the pages of my works coming
together in one neat, beautiful, poetry book.

And to the avid readers and lovers of poetry; I
hope my book was worth the read. I hope it sparks
discussions and open debates. I hope my words help,
in some way. Thank you for taking the time to read,
'My thinking, my lyrics, my songs, in the form of poems'.

Here's to kindness, courage and strength.
Love Lisa

www.ingramcontent.com/pod-product-compliance
Lightning Source LLC
LaVergne TN
LVHW040058080526
838202LV00045B/3704